AWAKENING The Investor Inside

"Mastering the Psychology of Wealth"

RAJAN UPADHYAY

Made with ❤ on the Notion Press Platform

www.notionpress.com

"To my late father, who taught me that true wealth is built on patience and character.And to the awakened investor inside us all."

Contents

Foreword

Let's be honest. For most people, the stock market feels like a cross between a high-stakes casino and a terrifying math exam you didn't study for. We are constantly bombarded with intimidating jargon—algorithmic hedging, derivatives, stochastic oscillators—that seems perfectly designed to make us feel small, keep us confused, and leave the "experts" in charge of our money.

Rajan didn't learn the mechanics of wealth by staring at blinking red and green screens in an air-conditioned trading room. He learned it in the engine room of the real world. Having spent over a decade elbow-deep in heavy industry, energy grids, and global supply chains, he understands how actual, tangible businesses make their money.

In *Awakening The Investor Inside*, Rajan takes the imposing fortress of Dalal Street and playfully dismantles it. He proves that the stock market isn't a casino at all—it is simply a grand, noisy, traditional Indian Bazaar. And once you know how to shop, the shouting stops being scary.

With sharp wit, brilliant analogies, and zero tolerance for financial nonsense, he bridges the gap between complex corporate realities and the everyday earner. He replaces the sweating anxiety of speculation with the calm, grounded logic of a true business owner. In these pages, you won't find fleeting "hot tips" or get-rich-quick schemes. Instead, you will learn how to spot the unbreakable "Toll Booths," how to safely walk past the "Snake Charmers," and how to cultivate the sheer, agonizing patience required to grow a generational "Mango Orchard."

Whether you are a young professional looking to deploy your first savings or a seasoned worker tired of feeling like an outsider to your own financial future, this book is a rare gift. It rewires your financial psychology from the ground up.

Pull up a chair and turn the page. The bazaar is open, the rules are finally in your favor, and you couldn't ask for a better guide.

PC Samantaray

May, 2026

Preface

“The financial industry thrives on a profitable illusion: that wealth creation requires complex algorithms and impenetrable jargon. In reality, the stock market is simply the ultimate business Bazaar, governed by the raw, fundamental laws of capital allocation and consumer demand.Drawing on over a decade of corporate experience analyzing the ground-level mechanics of heavy industry and supply chains, I wrote Awakening Investor Inside to bridge the gap between financial theory and practical reality. This book strips away the daily noise of Dalal Street, replacing the anxiety of speculation with the structured, analytical clarity of a true business owner.By mastering these proprietary mental models—from spotting structural "Toll Booths" to cultivating the patience of a "Mango Orchard"—you will no longer be a timid outsider. The mechanics of absolute wealth are hiding in plain sight.It is time to awaken the investor inside.

Rajan Upadhyay

2026

Acknowledgments

"Writing a book is a solitary act, but the wisdom within it is never self-made. This work is the culmination of shared experiences, hard-learned lessons, and unwavering support.To the colleagues and mentors from my years in the corporate world, across the manufacturing floors and boardrooms: thank you for showing me the unfiltered reality of how true businesses operate.To my father, whose endless support and quiet wisdom taught me that the foundation of any lasting wealth—in markets and in life—is built on character and patience. Your guidance has always been my compass.To my partner, thank you for standing by my side through the profound transition from the corporate grind to the rewarding, unpredictable world of entrepreneurship and investing. This book exists because of your belief in me.Finally, to you, the reader. Thank you for stepping into the bazaar."

Introduction

"Every morning, millions surrender their financial destiny to an illusion. They stare at screens flashing red and green, paralyzed by a financial language they do not speak. The industry bombards them with complex jargon—algorithmic hedging, derivatives, stochastic oscillators—designed with a singular purpose: to convince you that wealth creation is a dangerous casino reserved only for insiders.It is a highly profitable lie.Beneath the manufactured panic, Dalal Street is not a casino. It is simply a marketplace. It is the ultimate Indian Bazaar.During my decade navigating the engine room of the Indian economy—analyzing the heavy infrastructure of power generation and the complex logistics of global supply chains—I witnessed how enterprise wealth is actually manufactured. The rules that govern a billion-dollar monopoly are the exact same rules that dictate whether a local vendor succeeds. You do not need a finance degree to build a generational empire. You simply need the common sense you already possess, paired with a framework to translate the language of the bazaar."

"Awakening Investor Inside is that framework. In the chapters ahead, we will completely rewire your financial psychology, replacing the anxiety of speculation with the analytical clarity of a true business owner.You will learn the Physiology of Profit. I will show you how to walk past the noise and spot the invincible Toll Booths—the structural monopolies where every competitor is forced to pay a fee. You will learn to navigate the terrifying Great Monsoons of market crashes using the precise logic of the Ping-Pong Ball Valuation, and recognize the toxic gambling traps of the Snake Charmer's Flute that destroy novice portfolios. Ultimately, you will cultivate the Mango Orchard Mindset, mastering the absolute psychology of patience to let compounding do the heavy lifting while you sleep.You will not find a list of "hot tips" here. I absolutely do not give the verdict; I leave it entirely to the readers to research, evaluate, and decide. My objective is to hand you the Apprentice's Ledger—the exact mental models required to evaluate any business, in any market condition, for the rest of your life.The era of playing the timid outsider is over.Turn the page. The bazaar is open."

RAJAN UPADHYAY

8 May, 2026

Chapter 1-The Bazaar Beneath the Banyan Tree

Imagine walking into your local *sabzi mandi* (vegetable market) on a bustling Sunday morning. You hear the vendors shouting their prices, buyers negotiating for a better deal on tomatoes, and the general hum of energy as goods change hands. If a vendor has the only fresh batch of mangoes in the market, he can charge a premium. If ten vendors are selling the exact same potatoes, the price drops.

This simple exchange of supply and demand is the beating heart of the stock market.

To understand the Indian stock market, we have to travel back in time. Long before the blinking red and green screens of modern trading terminals, the market was a literal gathering of people. In the 1850s, a group of stockbrokers in Mumbai (then Bombay) used to gather under a sprawling Banyan tree in front of the Town Hall. As their numbers grew, they moved from beneath one leafy canopy to another, eventually settling on a street that would become famous worldwide: Dalal Street.

What started as a handful of men trading shares under a tree has evolved into a massive, digital ecosystem. But the core principle remains exactly the same as the local vegetable bazaar: it is simply a place where buyers and sellers meet to agree on a price. Instead of trading vegetables, they are trading tiny pieces of ownership in companies—from the Tata trucks you see on the highway to the Reliance network powering your phone.

However, to truly succeed as an investor, understanding the mechanics of buying and selling is only half the battle. The other half is understanding the market's **psychology**.

When we talk about the psychology of the market, we are talking about its behaviour, its reflexes, and its psychology. The stock market is not a cold, unfeeling machine. It breathes, reacts, panics, and celebrates. It is driven by two of the oldest human emotions: fear and greed.

When a company announces great news, greed takes over, and buyers rush in, pushing prices higher. When global events cause uncertainty, fear grips the crowd, and sellers dump their shares, sending prices crashing down. Just like a human body has a reflex to pull its hand away from a hot stove, the market has reflexes to economic changes, political shifts, and global news.

For a new investor, jumping into this environment can feel overwhelming. But if you learn to observe the market's psychology—if you learn to understand *why* the crowd is reacting the way it is—you stop being a victim of its mood swings. You learn to stay calm when everyone else is panicking, and you learn to be cautious when everyone else is blindly confident.

We are going to explore how this living, breathing bazaar works, so you can navigate its cycles and ultimately build lasting wealth.

Chapter 2: Is the Indian Stock Market Safe?

> "Behind every stock is a company. Find out what it's doing." — *Peter Lynch*

Understanding How It Works

A common question for beginners looking at the Indian stock market is: *Is my money safe?* We have all heard old stories about lost physical share certificates or shady middlemen. Because of these myths, the fear of losing money keeps many people away from wealth creation. But the truth is, the modern Indian share market is one of the most technologically advanced, highly regulated, and secure financial systems in the world.
To build your confidence as a new investor, you need to understand the structure of the market. Here is a simple breakdown of the key stakeholders who run, protect, and regulate the Indian stock market.

The Digital Supermarkets: BSE and NSE Explained

If the stock market is a giant bazaar, the BSE (Bombay Stock

Exchange) and the NSE (National Stock Exchange) are the two massive, secure digital supermarkets where the actual buying and selling happens.

BSE: The oldest stock exchange in Asia, which started under the famous Banyan tree in Mumbai.

NSE: The younger, highly computerized exchange that changed how digital trading works in India.

When you want to buy shares in a company, you do not buy directly from that company. You buy them through these stock exchanges. They provide the safe digital platforms that match buyers and sellers instantly and transparently.

The Digital Lockers: NSDL and CDSL (Where Are My Shares Stored?)

A major fear for new investors is: *What if the trading app I use shuts down? Will I lose my shares?* The answer is no. This is where NSDL (National Securities Depository Limited) and CDSL (Central Depository Services Limited) come in. Think of them as high-security digital lockers created by the government.

When you buy a share, it is converted into a digital format (stored in your Demat account) and kept safely in one of these two vaults. Your stockbroker does not actually hold your shares. Even if your broker goes out of business tomorrow, your investments remain 100% safe with NSDL or CDSL, permanently linked to your PAN card.

The Strict Umpire: What is SEBI?

A game is only fair if there is a strict umpire watching every move. In India, that umpire is SEBI (Securities and Exchange Board of India).

SEBI is the top government regulator of the financial markets. Its main job is simple: to protect retail investors like you. * Before a company can ask the public for money, SEBI checks its financial health.

SEBI sets strict rules for the stock exchanges (BSE/NSE) and stockbrokers.

It uses advanced technology to catch insider trading, scams, or price manipulation.

If anyone breaks the rules, SEBI issues massive fines and bans them from the market. Knowing that SEBI is watching 24/7 is what gives millions of Indian investors the confidence to invest.

The Ticket Counters: Stockbrokers

You cannot walk directly into the NSE or BSE to buy a share. You need an authorized agent, known as a stockbroker. These include popular apps like Zerodha, Groww, Upstox, or traditional bank brokers (like HDFC Securities or ICICI Direct).

Brokers are simply the entry gates. They provide the mobile apps and websites where you place your buy or sell orders. They send your order to the exchange for a very small fee, making the process fast and easy.

Summary: The Stock Market Safety Net

When you put all these pieces together, the Indian stock market structure is incredibly safe for beginners:

You use a **Stockbroker** to place an order.

The trade happens securely on the **NSE or BSE**.

Your shares are locked safely away in the government-backed vaults of **NSDL or CDSL**.

Watching over this entire process to ensure nobody cheats you is **SEBI**.

Your hard-earned money is not floating in a risky void. It moves through a secure, transparent, and strictly guarded system. With the fear of the market out of the way, you can now focus on the most important part of investing: understanding market psychology and choosing the right companies.

Chapter 3-The Detective in the Bazaar

Finding Multi-baggers in Plain Sight

When people think of stock market experts, they usually picture someone sitting in front of six computer screens, staring at complex technical charts with red and green lines zig-zagging everywhere. But some of the greatest wealth in the Indian stock market has been created by everyday people who simply walked out of their front doors, looked around, and connected the dots.

You do not need to be a math genius or know how to read technical analysis charts to find multi-bagger stocks (stocks that multiply your initial investment many times over). You just need to understand the psychology of a fundamental investor and learn how to observe the real world around you.

The Fundamental Investor's Psychology: Business Over Stock Tickers

A technical trader looks at a stock as a volatile line on a chart. A fundamental investor looks at a stock and sees a living, breathing business.

The psychology of fundamental investing is rooted in deep common sense. If a company makes a product that everyone around you is buying, the company will make a profit. If the company consistently grows its profit, its share value will eventually go up. The successful fundamental investor ignores the daily noise and shouting of the bazaar, focusing entirely on the quality of the product and future consumer demand.

The "Look Around You" Strategy for Finding Stocks
The easiest, most practical way to find great companies is simply to observe your daily life and ask "Why?".

Why are there suddenly new stickers at the local petrol pump mentioning "E20"?

What payment app is every local shopkeeper using?

What brand of shoes are college students wearing?

Behind every changing habit or new government mandate is a listed company facilitating it.

Live Indian Market Example

Praj Industries and the Ethanol Story

Let's look at a classic live example from the Indian equity market that perfectly combines everyday observation with government policy:

A few years ago, the Indian government faced a massive economic problem: the country was spending billions of dollars importing crude oil to run its vehicles, which was hurting the economy and creating massive pollution. To solve this, the government aggressively pushed the Ethanol Blended Petrol (EBP) program. They mandated that oil companies must mix ethanol (a biofuel made largely from sugarcane and agricultural waste) with regular petrol. If you were an observant investor, you might have noticed the news about helping sugarcane farmers, or seen the new blending targets (like E10 and E20) popping up at your local fuel station.

The fundamental investor asks:

If the entire country is suddenly mandated to produce millions of litres of ethanol, who builds the factories that make the ethanol?

The answer was Praj Industries, a global leader in bio-based technologies and engineering, headquartered right here in India. While the rest of the market was chasing popular tech stocks, Praj was quietly securing massive orders to build ethanol plants across the country.

Because they were perfectly positioned for this massive macroeconomic shift, their profits soared. The stock, which was quietly trading around the ₹50 to ₹70 range in early 2020, skyrocketed over the next few years, crossing the ₹500 to ₹600 marks. You didn't need to know technical analysis to catch this multi-bagger; you just needed to connect the government's pain point (costly oil imports) with the solution (ethanol) and find the company building the shovels for the gold rush.

The Contrarian Reflex: Why Buying the Market Panic Works

Here is where stock market psychology gets interesting. Once you find a great company using your observation skills, you do not always buy it immediately. You wait. The stock market is highly emotional. Sometimes, the overall market will panic because of global news that has nothing to do with the actual business of your chosen company. People sell their shares out of fear, driving the stock price down. This is the moment the educated observer steps in and grabs a wonderful business at a heavily discounted price. Warren Buffett famously calls this being "fearful when others are greedy, and greedy when others are fearful."

Connecting the Macroeconomic Dots: Finding Future Sectors

Looking at everyday consumer products and government mandates is the first step. The second, more powerful step is mastering Macroeconomics—which simply means following what the government is focusing on next and where the future economy is heading.

Let's look at another live situation playing out right now in the modern Indian economy:

Dot 1: The Electric Vehicle (EV) Revolution. Similar to the ethanol push, the government desperately wants to push EV adoption. If millions of cars shift to batteries, the country needs massive amounts of new electricity and EV charging stations.

Dot 2: The Artificial Intelligence (AI) Boom. The world is shifting toward AI. While the US creates the chips, India handles the backend IT infrastructure. Running AI requires giant Data Centres. What do Data Centres need to run 24/7 without melting down? Massive amounts of continuous electricity.

The Convergence: When you join these dots, a clear picture emerges. Both the EV revolution and the AI boom depend entirely on the Power Sector.

Live Example: The Power Sector Boom

Let's look at Tata Power as our practical example.

A few years ago, power companies were considered slow, boring businesses. But an investor who connected the macroeconomic dots realized that Tata Power was aggressively expanding its renewable green energy footprint and building thousands of EV charging stations across Indian highways. Because they were positioned perfectly for future demand, the stock transitioned from trading in the double digits a few years ago to trading around ₹435 by early 2026, becoming a massive wealth creator for those who saw the economic shift early.

Your Next Steps in the Bazaar

Once you have used your observation skills to find the right sector (whether it is Ethanol blending or Power generation), your job as the stock market detective narrows down. You no longer have to analyse 5,000 companies on the BSE or NSE. You only need to look at the specific sector and find the top 2 or 3 companies that are actively working on future-proof solutions.

By paying attention to the world, connecting the dots of government policy, and waiting for the right price, you have successfully done the work of a seasoned fundamental investor.

Chapter 4: Owning the Toll Booth

The Power of a Duopoly

In the previous chapter, we learned how to spot great companies by observing everyday life and connecting macroeconomic dots. But what if there was a way to make money regardless of which specific company or sector becomes the next big thing?

What if, instead of trying to pick the most profitable shop in the bazaar, you could simply own the gates to the bazaar itself?
To understand how this works, we must first understand one of the most powerful concepts in fundamental investing: The Duopoly.

What is a Duopoly Business?

In economics, a "monopoly" is a market where only one company has total control (like Indian Railways). A "duopoly" is a market where exactly two dominant companies control almost the entire industry.

Think about your daily life:

When you order food online, you use either **Zomato** or **Swiggy**.

When you look at your debit or credit card, it is likely powered by either **Visa** or **Mastercard**.

When you buy an airplane ticket in India, you are most likely flying with **IndiGo** or **Air India**.

Duopolies are a fundamental investor's dream. Why? Because starting a new company to compete with them is nearly impossible. They have what investors call a "Moat"—a deep, protective ditch around their business castle. In a duopoly, the two companies do not need to destroy each other with massive discounts; they simply divide the growing market between themselves and enjoy massive, consistent profits.

The Ultimate Indian Duopoly: The Stock Exchanges

Let's bring this back to our bazaar analogy. In Chapter 2, we discussed the two digital mega-malls where all shares in India are bought and sold: the BSE (Bombay Stock Exchange) and the NSE (National Stock Exchange). If an Indian citizen wants to buy a share of Tata Motors, Reliance, or HDFC Bank, that transaction must pass through either the BSE or the NSE. There is no third option. They hold a strict, SEBI-regulated duopoly over the Indian equity market. Every time a trade happens, the exchange collects a tiny toll tax.

As a fundamental investor, the psychology here is brilliant. You do not need to worry if Tata Motors beats Maruti Suzuki, or if HDFC Bank beats ICICI Bank. As long as people are trading their shares, the stock exchanges are making money.

The BSE Multi-bagger Case Study

While the NSE is the larger exchange by volume, it is currently an unlisted company (meaning the general public cannot easily buy its shares on the open market). This leaves the BSE as the only major listed stock exchange in India where retail investors can buy a piece of the business.
Let's look at the incredible wealth creation story of BSE Ltd.
The Setup (The Macroeconomic Dot): A few years ago, investing in the stock market was something only a small fraction of Indians did. But post-2020, India experienced a financial awakening. Armed with cheap internet, smartphones, and user-friendly broker apps, millions of young Indians entered the market. The number of Demat accounts in India skyrocketed from around 4 crore in 2020 to over 15 crore by early 2024, and the numbers kept climbing.

The Business Mechanics:

How did this benefit BSE?

Transaction Fees: More investors meant millions of more trades every single day.

Mutual Funds: BSE owns "BSE StAR MF," India's largest mutual fund routing platform. As the SIP (Systematic Investment Plan) culture boomed, BSE routed millions of these monthly investments, collecting a fee on each one.

F&O Expansion: BSE strategically relaunched its derivatives (Futures & Options) contracts, capturing a massive wave of trading volume that brought in explosive revenue.

The Wealth Creation (The Multi-bagger Result) Because BSE operates in a duopoly with incredibly high barriers to entry, it didn't have to spend billions fighting off new startup competitors. It just had to upgrade its technology and let the tsunami of new Indian investors wash over its toll booths.

The financial results were staggering. BSE's profits multiplied, and the stock market rewarded this growth heavily. An investor who recognized this duopoly moat a few years ago could have bought shares of BSE Ltd at adjusted prices of a few hundred rupees. By early 2026, driven by record profits and massive market participation, the BSE share price surged past the ₹3,400 to ₹3,500 mark, delivering returns of thousands of percent to its patient shareholders.

The Lesson for the Novice Investor

The BSE story is the perfect example of how avoiding the noise can make you wealthy.

Many traders exhaust themselves trying to predict which specific stock will go up 5% tomorrow. Meanwhile, the fundamental investor zooms out. They look for structural advantages—like a duopoly. They identify a toll booth that everyone has to pass through, buy a piece of it, and let the natural growth of the Indian economy do the heavy lifting for them.

Chapter 5-The Only Game in Town

Understanding Monopolies

In our last chapter, we explored the concept of a duopoly—a market ruled by two dominant players sharing the profits. But let us take our bazaar analogy one step further.

Imagine you are walking through the market in the scorching peak of Indian summer. You are incredibly thirsty. However, in this specific bazaar, the local municipality has passed a strict rule: only one specific vendor is legally allowed to sell drinking water. No one else can open a water stall.

If you want water, you have to buy it from him. He does not need to shout to attract customers. He does not need to offer discounts. He does not need to spend money on flashy signboards. He just sits there, and the customers come to him automatically.

In the stock market, this vendor is called a Monopoly.

What is a Monopoly Business?

A monopoly exists when a single company completely dominates an industry, leaving essentially zero room for competitors. While duopolies have a wide "moat" protecting their castle, monopolies have a massive, impenetrable wall. Usually, absolute monopolies in India exist because of strict government regulations, high capital requirements, or exclusive licensing.

Here are a few classic examples of monopoly or near-monopoly businesses in the Indian stock market:

Hindustan Aeronautics Limited (HAL): If the Indian Air Force needs new indigenous fighter jets or helicopters, they go to HAL. No private startup can easily start manufacturing fighter jets in their garage.

Coal India Limited: This massive government-owned entity controls the vast majority of coal production in the country, powering India's electricity grid.

Multi Commodity Exchange (MCX): Just like the BSE is a toll booth for equity shares, MCX is a near-monopoly toll booth for trading commodities like gold, silver, and crude oil in India.

For a fundamental investor, finding a monopoly feels like finding a goldmine. The company has pricing power, guaranteed customers, and incredibly high profit margins.

The Case Study: The IRCTC Wealth Engine

Perhaps the most famous and relatable monopoly in India is the Indian Railway Catering and Tourism Corporation (IRCTC).
If you have ever travelled on a train in India, you have been a customer of this company. IRCTC is a "Mini Ratna" government enterprise. Let's break down its business to understand why it is the ultimate monopoly:

Internet Ticketing: If you want to book a reserved train ticket online in India, there is only one gateway: IRCTC. Even if you use third-party apps like MakeMyTrip or Paytm, they are simply acting as agents; the ticket is still processed through the IRCTC servers, and IRCTC collects a convenience fee. They hold roughly a 100% monopoly on online railway ticketing.

Catering Services: When you are hungry on a long-distance Vande Bharat or Rajdhani train, IRCTC is the sole authorized entity to manage the pantry cars and food delivery.

Rail Neer: They are the exclusive provider of packaged drinking water on Indian trains and railway stations.

THE INVESTOR'S PSYCHOLOGY

from a fundamental investor's perspective, the beauty of IRCTC is its "asset-light" ticketing business. IRCTC does not own the actual trains, the tracks, or the stations. The Indian railways handles the heavy, expensive work of running the trains. IRCTC simply provides the digital gateway and collects the cash. Because it costs almost nothing extra to process 10,000 digital tickets versus 1,000 digital tickets, the profit margins are staggering.

When the company was listed on the stock exchanges, investors aggressively bought its shares. They recognized that as India's population grew and more people shifted from unreserved coaches to reserved ac coaches, IRCTC's profits would naturally multiply without them having to lift a finger. The stock became a massive multi-bagger, generating tremendous wealth for its early shareholders.

THE CATCH: THE "STROKE OF A PEN" RISK

if monopolies are so perfect, shouldn't a novice investor just put all their money into them?
Here is where stock market psychology requires caution. The biggest strength of an Indian monopoly is usually its biggest weakness: the government. Because the government grants the monopoly, they can also change the rules at any moment.

Let's look back at IRCTC for a practical lesson. In late 2021, IRCTC was earning hundreds of crores in pure profit from the "convenience fee" charged on every online ticket. One evening, the ministry of railways suddenly announced a new policy: IRCTC would have to share 50% of all its convenience fee revenue with the government.

The market panicked. The psychology shifted from extreme greed to extreme fear. The next morning, IRCTC's share price crashed by over 20%, wiping out roughly ₹20,000 crores in market value in a matter of days.

Note: The government withdrew the decision shortly after due to the massive backlash, and the stock recovered, but the lesson was permanently etched into the market.

THE TAKEAWAY FOR THE DETECTIVE IN THE BAZAAR

When you find a monopoly like IRCTC or HAL, you have found a phenomenal wealth-creating engine. The business economics are almost impossible to beat. However, as an intelligent investor, you must always remember that a monopoly's moat is often dug by government policy.

Enjoy the profits of the only water vendor in the bazaar, but always keep one eye on the municipality office to make sure they aren't changing the rules of the market.

Chapter 6: Weathering The Monsoon

Market Cycles & The Ping-Pong Ball

In our journey through the bazaar so far, you have learned how to spot the best stalls. You know how to find the detectives uncovering hidden gems, and you understand the unmatched power of the merchants who own the toll booths and run the only game in town.

But knowing what to buy is only half the battle. The other half—the half where most novice shoppers lose their hard-earned money—is knowing when to buy and how to handle the changing weather of the marketplace.

The stock market is a living, breathing entity. It is driven by human emotion, which means it has moods, rhythms, and seasons. To survive and thrive here, you cannot force the market to operate on your schedule or timeline. You must respect its livelihood. Let's begin by understanding the natural seasons of the bazaar.

The Rhythms Of The Bazaar (The Short-Term / Yearly Cycle)

If you stand in the middle of any grand Indian marketplace long enough, you will realize that the crowd does not move at the same speed all year round. The stock market is no different; it has a recognizable, short-term yearly cycle driven by culture, psychology, and the financial calendar.

The Diwali High

Think of the marketplace just before Diwali. The streets are strung with bright lights and marigold flowers. There is a chill in the air, but the atmosphere is warm with laughter, bonuses in pockets, and the auspicious spirit of mahurat trading. This cultural euphoria spills directly into the stock market. Traditionally, between November and January, the Indian market experiences a massive buying surge. Demand is high, optimism is everywhere, and as a collective result of this festive greed, prices are often pushed to their yearly peaks.

The Spring Cleaning

But no festival lasts forever. As February rolls in, the festive lights are taken down and the reality of the union budget sets in. Following this, the end of the financial year looms in march. The mood in the bazaar shifts. Merchants, fund managers, and big investors begin to balance their books, pay their advance taxes, and book the profits they made during the winter high. This period, from February to April, is the market's natural correction phase. Prices dip as the euphoria settles. It is the bazaar's annual spring cleaning.

The Summer Lull

Once the financial books are closed and the tax dust settles, the bazaar enters a quieter phase. From April to June, the market catches its breath. The chaotic shouting of the winter and the anxiety of the spring are replaced by a steady, quiet hum. This is the consolidation period. The market is establishing a new base, figuring out its footing before it gears up to attempt new highs later in the year.

The Global Winds

However, there is one crucial caveat every intelligent investor must remember: our bazaar does not have a roof. It is entirely exposed to the elements. While these seasonal patterns repeat often enough to be noticeable, they are never guaranteed. A sudden storm in another country—a geopolitical conflict, an oil crisis, or changing interest rates across the ocean—can act as a strong global wind, blowing our local bazaar completely off its usual course. You must respect the yearly cycle, but never treat it as a rigid calendar.

The Five-Year Reign (The Medium-Term / Election Cycle)

While the yearly seasons dictate the short-term mood of the bazaar, there is a heavier, more powerful rhythm playing in the background: the medium-term political cycle. Every five years, the nation holds its central elections. For the stock market, this five-year cycle dictates the flow of big capital.

The Policy Watch (Years 1 & 2)

When a new government takes charge (or begins a new term, like the 2024–2029 cycle), the first two years are often marked by caution. The big merchants—institutional investors and foreign funds—act like shopkeepers waiting to read the new tax laws before committing their money. They want to understand the government's approach toward the economy. Because of this hesitation, these first two years often serve as a natural correction or cooling-off period. Investor sentiment is cautious.

Finding the Footing (Years 2 & 3)

As the government's policies are rolled out and clarified, the market adjusts to the "new normal." The hesitation fades. This becomes the consolidation period, where the market builds a strong foundation based on actual economic growth rather than speculation.

The Election Rally (Years 4 & 5)

As the cycle enters its final years, the government typically increases spending, announces populist measures, and pushes infrastructure projects to woo voters before the next election. Optimism surges. This clarity and spending drive a massive wave of capital into the market, often resulting in a powerful rally that pushes indices to staggering new highs.

The Great Storms (The 10-Year Crisis Cycle)

You can master the yearly seasons and ride the five-year election cycles, but eventually, every investor must face the Great Monsoon.

The 30% Wipeout

Historically, every decade or so, a massive wealth-reset event shakes the global markets. We saw it during the 2008 Global Financial Crisis and again during the 2020 Corona Crisis. When these rare storms hit, absolute panic takes over Dalal Street. The Nifty and Sensex do not just dip; they plummet, often erasing 30% to 35% of their value in a matter of months.

Respecting the Market's Timeline

Novice investors often fall into the trap of looking at the calendar, expecting a crash exactly every ten years. But notice the 12-year gap between 2008 and 2020. You must respect the market's livelihood—it is a living entity, and it will always surprise you. It will not follow your strict timelines.

Preparation over Prediction

The goal of understanding this 10-year cycle is not to predict the exact Tuesday the market will crash. It is about knowing what to expect so you do not panic. It is about knowing when to be cautious, and understanding at what percentage drops you need to be ready to aggressively buy.

This brings us to the most important mental model an investor can possess. To understand why the market crashes so violently—and why it recovers just as aggressively—you need to understand the forces of valuation.

The Ping-Pong Ball on a String (Understanding Valuation)

Imagine a simple toy: a ping-pong ball attached exactly to the middle of a thick rubber string, suspended vertically inside a wooden frame.

This ping-pong ball represents the stock market.

The Resting Middle (Actual Valuation)

When the bazaar is calm and no extreme emotions are acting upon it, the ball rests perfectly in the middle of the frame. This resting point is the market's Actual Valuation. In the real world, we measure this "resting point" using the P/E (Price-to-Earnings) ratio of the index. It represents what the businesses in the market are genuinely, fundamentally worth based on their profits.

The Upward Force (The Bulls)

Now, imagine grabbing that ping-pong ball and pulling it straight up toward the top of the frame. The rubber string stretches tight. This upward force is positive sentiment—the Bulls. During times of extreme greed (like a massive Diwali rally or the peak of a bull market), investors are so euphoric they will pay any price for a stock. They pull the market's price far above its actual resting valuation. But look at the string: it is strained. It defies gravity, but it cannot stay stretched forever. Eventually, the buying exhausts itself, and the market snaps back down to reality.

The Downward Force (The Bears)

Now, imagine grabbing the ball and pulling it violently downward, stretching the string to its absolute breaking point near the bottom of the frame. This is negative sentiment—the Bears during a Great Storm like 2008 or 2020.

Panic pulls the market down, down, down. It stretches the market's price far below its true, fundamental value. The news channels will scream that the economy is finished. They will tell you the rubber string is going to snap and the ball will fall into an endless abyss.

The V-Shaped Recovery

But the string rarely breaks. The further the market is pulled downward by extreme fear, the more violent the stored energy in that rubber string becomes. A 30% to 35% drop means the string is stretched to its absolute, maximum limit.

What happens when the panic finally exhausts itself? What happens when the sellers run out of shares to sell, and the extreme fear simply fades? You let go of the ball.

Snap. The ball rockets upward in a blur. It springs violently back toward its actual valuation, often overshooting it entirely. This is the V-shaped recovery. The harder the downward pull of fear, the faster and more aggressive the snap-back to reality.

The Strategy for the Storm

Armed with the knowledge of the ping-pong ball, you no longer need to fear the Great Monsoon. You simply need a shopping list.

When the market drops 10%, the string is beginning to stretch. You deploy a little cash and buy high-quality businesses at a discount.

When the market drops 20%, the fear on the street is deafening. You ignore the noise, take out more cash, and buy with conviction.

And if the market ever drops 30% to 35%, you know the ping-pong ball is stretched to its absolute limit. While the novices are paralyzed by terror, the awakened investor aggressively buys the fear, knowing that the violent, V-shaped snap-back is just a matter of time.

Case Study: The Master Builder and the Great Monsoon (Larsen & Toubro)

To truly understand how the ping-pong ball of valuation works during a crisis, we do not need to look at textbooks. We only need to look at recent history in our own Dalal Street bazaar. Let us examine one of the greatest wealth-creation opportunities born out of extreme fear: the story of Larsen & Toubro (L&T) during the 2020 Corona Crisis.

The Master Builder

Larsen & Toubro is not just a company; it is the master builder of India. If you see a massive airport, a metro line, a nuclear reactor, or a defence submarine being built in the country, there is a high probability L&T is behind it. It is a fundamental pillar of the Indian economy with an order book worth hundreds of thousands of crores. In January 2020, before the crisis hit, L&T was trading confidently near its peak around the ₹1,370 mark. The bazaar recognized its value, its near-monopoly in executing mega-scale infrastructure projects, and its solid leadership. The ping-pong ball was resting comfortably, perhaps stretching slightly upward with optimism.

The Great Monsoon Strikes

Then came March 2020. The Corona crisis swept across the globe, bringing with it lockdowns, uncertainty, and absolute terror. The Indian marketplace went into a state of panic rarely seen in a generation.

For a construction and engineering giant like L&T, the news was catastrophic. Laborers were migrating back to their villages. Factories were shuttered. Supply chains were completely broken. The news channels declared that infrastructure development in India would be stalled for a decade.

The Bears took hold of the ping-pong ball and pulled it down with violent force. The stock price of L&T, which had been flying high at ₹1,370, went into a terrifying freefall. Within weeks—hitting peak panic around late March 2020—the price crashed to an absolute low near ₹700. Nearly 50% of the master builder's market value had been wiped out in a matter of days.

The Illusion of the Stretched String

At ₹700, the novice investor looked at L&T and saw a dying company. They sold their shares at massive losses, convinced that the world was ending and the stock would go to zero.

But the awakened investor looked at the exact same situation and asked a different question: Did L&T suddenly lose half of its actual, intrinsic value? Did their heavy machinery disappear? Did their engineering patents vanish? Did the engineers forget how to build? Did the Indian government suddenly decide it would never build another road or airport again?

The answer was no. The fundamental business was bruised, but it was not broken. The massive drop from ₹1,370 to ₹700 was not a reflection of L&T's actual worth; it was the rubber string being stretched to its absolute, agonizing limit by extreme human fear. The market had severely underpriced the master builder.

The Violent Snap-Back

As we learned in the bazaar, the string rarely breaks. By late 2020 and into 2021, the extreme fear began to exhaust itself. The lockdowns eased, labourers returned, and the government—fitting perfectly into the medium-term cycle—began heavily pumping money into infrastructure to revive the economy.

The Bears Let Go Of The Ping-Pong Ball

The snap-back was ferocious. L&T didn't just recover to its pre-COVID ₹1,370 levels; it rocketed past them. As the government's capital expenditure grew and L&T's order book swelled to record highs, the stock price climbed year after year.

Today, that same stock trades confidently around the ₹4,000 mark.

The Intelligent Shopper's Lesson

Let's look at the math of fear and conviction. The novice who bought at the pre-crisis peak of ₹1,370 and sold in panic at ₹700 destroyed half their wealth. They let the monsoon dictate their actions. But the awakened investor who understood the ping-pong ball saw the crash as a generational clearance sale. An investor who bravely deployed their capital and bought L&T around the ₹700 to ₹800 levels during the peak of the fear in March 2020 has now seen their capital multiply more than five times over (a 400%+ return) as the price reached ₹4,000.

They did not do this by reading complex charts. They did it through simple investing psychology: they bought an incredible business when the rubber string of fear was stretched to its limit, and they patiently waited for reality to snap back.

Chapter 7: The Snake Charmer's Flute & The Mango Orchard

Investing Psychology Explained

You have walked far through the Dalal Street bazaar. You now know how to spot the toll booths and the monopolies. You know how to find the hidden gems, and you understand how to weather the great monsoons by respecting the ping-pong ball of valuation.

But knowing what to buy and when to buy it is only the beginning. The final, and arguably most difficult, test for the beginner investor is managing their own behaviour after the purchase is made. To build generational wealth in the Indian stock market, you must learn to avoid the traps of greed and master the agonizing psychology of patience.

The Snake Charmer's Flute: The Danger of Penny Stocks

As you walk away from the grand, brightly lit storefronts of the trusted merchants, you will inevitably hear a whisper from a dark alleyway of the bazaar.

A stranger leans in, eyes wide, and says, "Pssssst... I have a secret. There is a small, broken-down stall in the back selling shares for just ₹1. By next Diwali, it will be worth ₹10. A ten-bagger! Put your money here, and you will become a crorepati overnight."

This is the Snake Charmer's Flute. It plays a hypnotic tune of pure greed that strikes directly at the novice investor's heart. Your mind instantly starts doing the thrilling math: "If I buy 10,000 shares at ₹1, it only costs me ₹10,000! If it hits ₹10, I've made a lakh! What's the harm in taking a small chance on a penny stock?"

Before you hand over your hard-earned money, you must understand the brutal psychology hiding behind this transaction.

The "Sleep-Tight" Test for Beginners

Deep down in your gut, you already know this ₹1 stock is a gamble. How do we know? Because of the amount you chose to invest. You only risked ₹10,000. You tell yourself it's "play money" or a "lottery ticket."

Now, ask yourself a difficult question: Would you put ₹5 Lakhs of your family's savings into that same ₹1 penny stock?

Your heart would instantly scream, "Absolutely not!" Your sleep would be destroyed. You would wake up sweating at 3:00 AM, checking your phone in terror, wondering if the promoters have run away or if the company has gone bankrupt overnight.

The Blue-Chip Fortress of Conviction

Now, look back at the main street of the bazaar. Look at the massive, unshakeable fortresses built by the Tatas, Reliance, or HDFC. These are blue-chip stocks—businesses whose products you use every single day. They have survived wars, economic crashes, and pandemics.

If someone tells you to slowly accumulate shares of Reliance on every market dip until you have ₹5 Lakhs invested, your heart feels completely different. Your pulse does not race. You can sleep like a baby. You know that even if the market catches a cold tomorrow, these giants will still be standing ten years from now.

You Cannot Spend Percentages

(Penny Stocks vs. Blue-Chip Returns)

Let's do the real math of wealth creation:

The Penny Gamble: You risk your ₹10,000. Let us assume a miracle happens, and the stock actually goes up 10 times (a 1,000% return). You now have ₹1 Lakh. You feel like a genius! But let's be honest: does ₹1 Lakh permanently change your life trajectory? Does it buy your dream home or secure your retirement? No.

The Blue-Chip Fortress: You invest ₹5 Lakhs into a steady, dominant business because you have the psychological conviction to do so without fear. Over the years, the business compounds quietly. Eventually, the stock doubles (a 100% return). Your ₹5 Lakhs is now ₹10 Lakhs.

Look at the difference. The penny stock gave you a thrilling 1,000% return, but the boring blue-chip created ten times more actual wealth. Wealth is not created by the percentage jump of a tiny bet. It is created by the size of the capital you have the psychological capacity to keep invested. You cannot take percentages to the grocery store. You buy houses and fund retirements with absolute rupees.

An investment you cannot sleep with is not an investment—it is a stress test.

The Mango Orchard: The Psychology of Patience and Compounding

Once you have safely avoided the snake charmers and bought shares in wonderful, fortress-like businesses, you face your final challenge: doing absolutely nothing.

Novice investors treat the stock market like a seasonal cash crop. They plant a seed on Monday and dig it up on Friday to see if the roots have grown. They constantly buy and sell, trading in and out of the bazaar, paying heavy taxes and brokerage fees along the way.

But true wealth is not a fast-cash crop. It is a Mango Orchard.

You can buy the finest mango seeds in the bazaar, plant them in the richest soil, and water them perfectly. But you cannot scream at the soil to make the tree grow faster. You cannot pull on the sapling to stretch it. You must let time do the heavy lifting.

This introduces the eighth wonder of the world:

The Power of Compounding-

It is simply money making money. In the early years of your orchard, the growth seems painfully slow. The trees are small. The dividends are tiny. The novice gets bored and chops the tree down to plant something else.

But the awakened investor embraces the boredom. They know that if they leave the orchard alone, the roots deepen. In year five, the tree bears a little fruit. By year ten, the branches are heavy. By year twenty, the orchard is so massive that it produces more fruit in a single season than the investor could have ever bought with their original capital.

The Intelligent Basket: The Power of SIPs (Systematic Investment Plans)

How do you actually build this orchard without losing your mind to the daily noise of the market? You use a Systematic Investment Plan (SIP).

You do not need to time the market perfectly. You do not need to guess the exact day the monsoon will hit. Instead, you visit the bazaar with an Intelligent Basket.

Every single month, on the exact same day, you put a set amount of money into your chosen fortress businesses or an index fund.

When the market is euphoric and prices are high, your fixed amount buys fewer shares.

When the market is terrified during a crash and prices are low, your fixed amount automatically buys more shares at a steep discount.

This simple, robotic habit completely removes human emotion from the equation. It stops you from acting on fear and greed. It ensures you are constantly accumulating high-quality assets while you sleep peacefully, letting the magic of compounding turn your monthly savings into a generational empire.

📦 THE AWAKENED INVESTOR'S LEDGER:

Core Takeaways

The Sleep-Tight Rule: If you are terrified to put a meaningful amount of your savings into a stock, your heart is telling you that you do not trust the business. Listen to it.

Percentages Don't Pay Bills: A 1,000% return on a tiny ₹5,000 gamble creates far less wealth than a boring 100% return on a ₹5 Lakh investment in a blue-chip stock. Focus on the absolute wealth you can confidently hold.

Plant an Orchard, Not a Cash Crop: True wealth requires agonizing patience. Buy phenomenal businesses and endure the boredom of doing absolutely nothing while compounding does the work.

Automate Your Bravery with SIPs: Use SIPs to systematically buy into the market every month. It removes the stress of "timing" the bazaar and naturally buys more shares when the market is cheap.

Chapter 8: The Apprentice's Ledger

Spotting Tomorrow's Giants

You have reached the final street of the Dalal Street bazaar. You now possess the tools of the awakened investor. You know how to identify the toll booths and monopolies. You know how to connect the macroeconomic dots. You understand the natural, seasonal rhythms of market crashes, and you know how to ignore the snake charmer's flute. But reading about the Indian stock market is very different from actually spending your money in it.

This final chapter is not a lesson; it is an exercise. To put everything you have learned into practice, let us take our magnifying glass and look at two real-world merchants currently operating in the bazaar. We will run them through the mental models we built in our book to perform a real-world SWOT analysis.

Grab your ledger. Let us look at tomorrow's giants.

Case Study 1: The Master Toolmaker

Mos Chip Technologies

The Narrative: The Architect of the Bazaar

In our bazaar, most shops sell grain, cloth, or spices. But there is one secluded workshop where the master artisans design the very scales used to weigh the grain and the looms used to weave the cloth. These are the Semiconductor Designers. They don't just follow the crowd; they create the blueprints for the future.

Usually, the bazaar prices a shop based on how much grain it sold yesterday. But what happens if this master weaver develops a new, unbreakable silk that only his loom can produce? The bazaar will no longer price his workshop based on last month's sales. They will price it based on the vision that every silk merchant will eventually need his tools.

Sector Positioning: The Digital Backbone

The Sector: Semiconductor & Product Engineering.

The Transformation: India is shifting from being a consumer of chips to a designer and manufacturer. Mos Chip is one of the few listed Indian players with the "end-to-end" capability to design complex Application-Specific Integrated Circuits (ASICs).

Economic Tailwind: The company is riding the wave of the India Semiconductor Mission and recent PLI (Production Linked Incentive) schemes. Delivering custom SoCs (System on Chips) to institutions like ISRO proves they are operating in high-stakes, high-entry-barrier territory.

The SWOT Analysis

Strengths:

- End-to-End Capabilities: Over 25 years of experience in silicon and AI engineering.
- Strategic Ecosystem: Strong foothold in software-driven hardware design and training infrastructure.
- Debt Profile: Strong financial risk profile with very low reliance on external debt.

Weaknesses:

- Talent War: High employee costs due to the global shortage of skilled VLSI engineers.
- Margin Volatility: Operating margins can fluctuate as the company prioritizes aggressive top-line growth over immediate profitability.
- Client Concentration: Success often depends on winning a few massive, complex global contracts.

The "Visionary Valuation" Paradigm: Writing a New Story

As of early 2026, Mos Chip has traded at valuation multiples (P/E ratios) well over 100x. A traditional accountant looking strictly at the current ledger might immediately dismiss this as "too expensive." However, a forward-looking investor must ask: Is the market pricing in a completely new story?

The Earnings Inflection Point: Historically, Mos Chip was a labour-intensive service business. Now, they are creating their own Intellectual Property (IP). In the semiconductor world, owning IP is like owning a master recipe—you can sell it a thousand times without adding more staff. High valuations often precede the moment when revenue scales exponentially while costs remain flat.

The Sovereign Moat: As the government prioritizes domestic design for defence and space, the "premium" on this stock is not just for its current profits; it is a premium paid for scarcity and strategic importance.

The Apprentice's Dilemma: A Seed for the Orchard?

We have looked at the workshop. We see the master artisans building the brains for satellites and the edge-AI of tomorrow. We also see the hefty price tag the bazaar has placed on their door. An expensive seed that grows into a massive Banyan tree is a better deal than a cheap seed that never sprouts—but it also carries the risk of high expectations. When observing this corner of the bazaar, one must ask: Would I rather own the shop that sells the fruit, or the workshop that makes the tools for every orchard in the land?

The evidence is before you. The research is now yours to complete.

Case Study 2: The Sovereign Shield

Bharat Dynamics Limited

The Narrative: The Armorer of the Bazaar

In every bustling bazaar, merchants focus on buying and selling their daily goods. But who protects the marketplace? In the quiet outskirts of the bazaar sits the Royal Armorer. For decades, the bazaar imported its shields and guards from distant lands at a heavy premium. Now, the decree has been made that the armorer must forge the defences locally. This armorer isn't just making a single sword; they are building the fortress that allows every other merchant to sleep peacefully and trade safely.

Sector Positioning: The Moat of National Security

The Sector: Defence Manufacturing (Guided Missiles and Underwater Weapons).

The Transformation: India is undergoing a historic shift from being one of the world's largest defence importers to becoming a self-reliant defence manufacturer and emerging exporter.

Economic Tailwind: BDL is a primary beneficiary of the government's Atmanirbhar Bharat (Self-Reliant India) initiative. With phased embargoes placed on importing specific defence equipment, the domestic order book for indigenous systems (like the Akash and Astra missiles) is locked in for years to come.

The SWOT Analysis

Strengths

- Monopoly Position: The sole manufacturer of surface-to-air and anti-tank guided missiles for the Indian armed forces
- Massive Visibility: A multi-year, multi-billion-dollar order book that provides highly predictable future revenue.

Weaknesses

- Client Concentration: Almost entirely dependent on a single buyer: The Ministry of Defence.
- Execution Risks: Bureaucratic delays, supply chain bottlenecks for specific imported sub-components, or delayed testing can push revenues into future quarters.

Opportunities

- The Export Horizon: Shifting from a strictly domestic supplier to exporting defence systems to friendly foreign nations, which carries much higher profit margins.

Threats

- Technological Obsolescence: Defence technology evolves rapidly. Failing to invest heavily in continuous R&D could lead to outdated weapon systems.

The "Visionary Valuation" Paradigm: Pricing the Fortress

When examining BDL, an apprentice investor might balk at the premium valuation multiples. If they look at the stall's current daily sales, the price might seem completely disconnected from reality. But here is where the "Visionary Valuation" comes into play:

Pricing the Order Book, Not the Quarter: The market is not valuing BDL on what it sold in the last three months. It is valuing a massive, contracted order book that stretches years into the future. This revenue isn't a hopeful guess; it is guaranteed by the sovereign government.

The Export Multiplier: Historically, BDL built solely for domestic use. The market is now pricing in the "New

Story" of BDL as a global defence exporter. Export orders bring higher margins and global prestige, fundamentally changing the company's financial profile from a domestic utility to a global competitor.

The Apprentice's Dilemma: A Seed for the Orchard?

We have inspected the armorer's forge. We know the mandate is clear: all future shields must be bought from this very workshop, and neighbouring kingdoms are now asking to buy these shields as well. Yet, the price to buy a stake in the forge today reflects all of this anticipated future success. When observing this corner of the bazaar, the author asks himself: Would I rather bet my ledger on the merchants trading everyday goods, or own a piece of the fortress that guarantees the bazaar's very survival? The evidence is before you. The research is now yours to complete.

Case Study 3: The Grand Counting House

Netweb Technologies

The Narrative: The Scribes of the New Age
In the bazaar, speed and foresight are everything. The merchants who can calculate their trades the fastest, and predict the weather for the mango orchard the most accurately, are the ones who thrive. For centuries, the bazaar relied on human scribes with simple ledgers. But now, a new architecture is rising: a massive, silent fortress of mathematics—a Grand Counting House. This building does not just record trades; it processes millions of data points a second to predict what the bazaar will demand tomorrow. Netweb is the master architect building these counting houses. They do not sell the grain; they build the absolute mathematical infrastructure that allows the modern bazaar to function.

Sector Positioning: The Sovereign Brain

The Sector: High-End Computing Solutions (HCS) and AI Infrastructure.

The Transformation: The world is undergoing an Artificial Intelligence revolution, requiring massive amounts of physical computing power. India is pivoting toward "Sovereign AI"—building its own indigenous supercomputing clusters rather than renting computing power from overseas servers.

Economic Tailwind: Supported by national initiatives and a booming corporate demand for data processing, Netweb stands as a leading Indian Original Equipment Manufacturer (OEM). By early 2026, their deployment of 'Make in India' AI supercomputing systems, powered by global giants like NVIDIA, positions them directly in the path of a historic capital expenditure cycle.

The SWOT Analysis

Strengths

- Indigenous OEM Leader: Rare end-to-end capability in India to design, manufacture, and deploy bespoke supercomputers and high-performance storage.
- Hyper-Growth Momentum: Incredible financial velocity, with recent quarters (like late 2025) showing top-line revenue growth exceeding 140% year-on-year.

Weaknesses

- Supply Chain Dependency: High reliance on imported global silicon (like specialized GPUs and CPUs) makes them vulnerable to global supply bottlenecks.

Opportunities

- The Enterprise AI Boom: Expanding from government/defence contracts (like ISRO) into private enterprises that desperately need their own AI and private cloud setups.

Threats

- Global Goliaths: Intense competition from massive, heavily capitalized multinational IT hardware companies seeking a piece of the Indian market.

The "Visionary Valuation" Paradigm: Pricing the Pick and Shovel

Netweb's valuation has historically commanded a massive premium, with P/E ratios frequently hovering well into the triple digits (100x to 130x) in 2026. A traditional investor, strictly reading the "Apprentice's Ledger," might immediately step away, viewing the stall as dangerously overpriced. But the "Future-Ready" investor looks at the mechanics of a gold rush.

The "Pick and Shovel" Premium: During a gold rush, the people who take on the most risk are those digging for gold (the software companies trying to build the next big AI app). The people who get rich safely are those selling the picks and shovels. Netweb is selling the shovels. The market is pricing in the reality that regardless of which software wins, they will all require Netweb's hardware to run.

The Sovereign Trust Multiplier: As data security becomes a matter of national defence, institutions are willing to pay a premium for an indigenous player they can trust. The valuation reflects an anticipated monopoly on domestic intelligence infrastructure.

The Apprentice's Dilemma: A Seed for the Orchard? We have stood outside the Grand Counting House. We can hear the hum of the machines inside processing the future. Its ledgers are overflowing with multi-million-dollar contracts, and its growth is undeniable. But the price to buy a single brick in this building today assumes it will become the undisputed central nervous system of the entire kingdom. When observing this stall, one must ask: Is it safer to bet on the merchants trying to outsmart each other, or to own the infrastructure that powers all of their thinking? The evidence is before you. The research is now yours to complete.

Case Study 4:The Alchemist's Evolution

Solar Industries

The Narrative: The Fire-Maker of the Bazaar For decades, there was a merchant in the bazaar who sold blasting powder. The builders bought it to clear land for roads, and the miners bought it to extract coal. It was a steady, predictable trade. But one day, the merchant realized that the same chemistry used to break rocks could be refined to propel the King's arrows into the sky.

The Fire-Maker stopped just selling raw powder and began engineering advanced rockets, guided defences, and mechanical birds (drones). The bazaar still sees him as the old blasting-powder merchant, but his workshop has quietly become the most critical armoury in the kingdom.

Sector Positioning: From Earth to Orbit

The Sector: Industrial Explosives transitioning to Aerospace & Defence Manufacturing.

The Transformation: Solar Industries is undergoing a radical metamorphosis. It is pivoting from a cyclical, volume-driven mining explosives company into a deep-tech, high-margin defence and space manufacturer.

Economic Tailwind: Benefiting massively from the government's defence indigenization push (Atmanirbhar Bharat), the company is not just making traditional munitions. As of early 2026, they are building propellants for ISRO and private space companies, and investing a massive ₹128 billion in a state-of-the-art Robotics and UAV (Unmanned Aerial Vehicle) facility in Nagpur.

The SWOT Analysis

Strengths

- Vertical Integration: They control the entire supply chain, from manufacturing raw high-energy materials to integrating the final rocket or drone.
- Massive Revenue Visibility: They possess a multi-year order book heavily skewed toward high-margin defence contracts (rockets, missiles, and loitering munitions like the Vijayastra).

Weaknesses

- Base Business Cyclicality: Despite the defence pivot, a portion of their revenue is still tied to the cyclical nature of mining and infrastructure.

- Execution Risk: Transitioning into cutting-edge domains like AI-driven swarm drones and space propellants carries high technical and regulatory execution risks.

Opportunities

- The Export Horizon: Rising global geopolitical tensions have created a severe worldwide shortage of artillery shells and munitions, opening a massive export market.

Threats

- Technological Shifts: The rapid evolution of electronic warfare and counter-drone technologies could render certain products obsolete if R&D lags.

The "Visionary Valuation" Paradigm: Pricing the Pivot

When an apprentice looks at the valuation of Solar Industries in 2026, they will see multiples that look alarmingly high for a "mining explosives" company. But the market is not pricing in a mining company; it is pricing in a Category Creator.

The Margin Expansion: Selling bulk explosives to a coal mine is a low-margin, high-volume business. Selling a proprietary loitering munition or a space-grade rocket propellant is a high-margin, high-IP business. The market is pricing in this radical shift in profitability.

The Private Space Race: As India opens its space sector to private players, Solar Industries is positioned as the premier "propulsion partner." A high valuation is the bazaar's way of pricing in an industry (private space tech) that barely existed five years ago.

The Apprentice's Dilemma: A Seed for the Orchard? We have looked into the Alchemist's workshop. We see the shift from breaking rocks to piercing the sky. We see the multi-billion rupee investments into the robotic warfare of the future. But we also see a price tag that leaves no room for the Alchemist to make a mistake.

When looking at this stall in the bazaar, the author asks himself: Am I willing to pay a premium today for a business that is shedding its old skin and attempting to become the kingdom's premier architect of aerospace and defence?

The evidence is before you. The research is now yours to complete.

Case Study 5: The Invisible Porter

Eternal Limited

The Narrative: The Invisible Porter of the Bazaar

In the old days of the bazaar, if you wanted hot food, you walked to the cookhouse. If you wanted fresh groceries, you walked to the grocer. But recently, a new force has taken over the marketplace: The Invisible Porter.

At first, this porter only ran meals from the cookhouses to your home. The traditional merchants laughed, calling him a mere delivery boy. But while they were laughing, the porter was mapping every alley, optimizing every route, and learning exactly what the people wanted and when they wanted it. Soon, he started delivering groceries in minutes. Then, he began supplying the raw ingredients to the cookhouses themselves. He stopped being a delivery boy and quietly became the indispensable blood-flow of the entire bazaar.

Sector Positioning: The Last-Mile Highway

The Sector: E-Commerce, Quick Commerce, and Consumer Tech.

The Transformation: Formerly known to the world as Zomato, the company rebranded to "Eternal Limited" to reflect its massive evolution. It is no longer just a food-delivery app; it is a sprawling "Commerce Ecosystem" encompassing food (Zomato), instant grocery delivery (Blinkit), B2B restaurant supplies (Hyperpure), and lifestyle/event ticketing (District).

Economic Tailwind: The company is capitalizing on the "Premiumization of Time." As India's urban middle class grows wealthier, their time becomes more valuable than minor price differences. Quick commerce is radically disrupting traditional retail by offering extreme convenience.

The SWOT Analysis

Strengths

- The Logistics Moat: An unparalleled, technology-driven logistics network spanning across India, creating massive barriers to entry for new players.
- Ecosystem Synergy: Vertically integrated operations capture both the B2C consumer wallet and the B2B supply chain, creating

multiple revenue streams from a single ecosystem.

Weaknesses

- Hyper-Competition: The quick-commerce space is ruthlessly competitive and requires continuous capital expenditure to build and maintain neighbourhood "dark stores."
- Margin Sensitivity: Despite crossing into profitability, overall profit margins remain highly sensitive to fuel costs, delivery fleet wages, and platform fee adjustments.

Opportunities

- The Total Urban Wallet: Expanding into out-of-home lifestyle services captures a larger share of the discretionary spending of the "time-poor, cash-rich" urbanite.

Threats

- Conglomerate Disruption: The looming threat of massive, deep-pocketed traditional conglomerates deciding to heavily subsidize their own entry into the quick-commerce wars.

The "Visionary Valuation" Paradigm: Pricing the Toll Bridge

When an apprentice looks at Eternal's valuation, they will see multiples that defy traditional accounting—often trading at a

P/E ratio exceeding 1000x. If judged strictly as a restaurant aggregator, this price is absurd. But the market is pricing in a completely different reality:

The Winner-Takes-Most Premium: The market believes that in the logistics of extreme convenience, there will only be one or two survivors. Investors are paying a massive premium today for the belief that Eternal is building an absolute digital monopoly over urban consumption.

Pricing the Toll Bridge: If you want a product delivered to an Indian home in 10 minutes, you must travel across Eternal's infrastructure. The valuation reflects the belief that eventually, almost every modern retail transaction in the city will require paying a tiny "toll" to this invisible porter.

The Apprentice's Dilemma: A Seed for the Orchard? We have watched the porter run through the bazaar. We have seen him grow from a startup burning cash to an ecosystem generating structural profit. We see that the citizens of the bazaar are completely addicted to the convenience he provides. But we also see a price tag so high that it demands absolute, flawless execution for years to come.

When observing this humming network in the bazaar, the author asks himself: Am I willing to pay a steep price for the Invisible Porter today, believing that tomorrow, no gold will change hands in the city without him taking a sliver of the coin?

The evidence is before you. The research is now yours to complete.

Conclusion

The Gates of the Bazaar

As we reach the edge of the bazaar, the noise of the shouting merchants, the clinking coins, and the frantic bargaining begins to fade. You came here as an apprentice, perhaps overwhelmed by the chaos. But now, as you look back at the winding alleys, you no longer see just a loud marketplace. You see the physiology of business. You see the toolmakers, the armorers, the fire-makers, and the invisible porters.

You have learned that investing is not about predicting the future; it is about finding the businesses that are building it. You have learned that a high price today might just be the cost of tomorrow's dominance, and that the internal ledger of your own mind is far more important than the fluctuating prices on a broker's screen.

But remember the golden rule of the mango orchard: The seed does not bear fruit the day it is planted. I have walked you through the stalls. I have shown you how to inspect the goods, how to question the merchants, and how to spot a stall that is writing a new story for the kingdom. But I will not tell you which seeds to buy. That verdict is not mine to give. The ultimate power of an awakened investor lies in their own conviction.

Before you step fully into the market, ask yourself these final questions:

Am I buying this business for what it did yesterday, or for what it will do tomorrow?

Does this company have a moat deep enough to keep the competitors at bay?

Do I have the patience to sit under the tree while the market storms rage around me?

The bazaar is now open. Your ledger is blank. The sun is high over the orchard.

The next entry is yours to write.

Epilogue

A Glimpse Over the Horizon

The Shared Orchards

Perhaps you have walked through this bazaar, learned the nature of the seeds, and realized something profound: I understand the value of the orchard, but I do not want to be the one inspecting every seed.

Many awakened investors look at the sheer effort required to analyse the stalls and feel a sense of hesitation. You might be a doctor, an engineer, a teacher, or a busy parent. You want to build generational wealth, but you fear the volatility of picking individual stalls. You do not want to spend your evenings deciphering balance sheets, yet you still want your money to work as hard as you do.

If you are wondering, "Is there a way to own the growth of the entire bazaar without the anxiety of choosing the right stall?"—the answer is a resounding yes.

In the upcoming Part 2 of the Awakening Investor Inside, we will leave the individual stalls behind and walk into the Shared Orchards.

We will demystify the multi-trillion-rupee world of the Mutual Fund Industry. You will learn:

The Master Gardeners: How to hire the brightest minds in the financial world to manage your wealth for a fraction of a percent.

The Shield of Diversification: How buying a broad basket of businesses protects your capital from the ruin of a single bad seed.

The Law of the Scales (The Risk-Reward Trade-off): In the bazaar, absolute safety and wild fortunes walk on opposite sides of the street. We will explore why, by choosing the protection of the shared orchard, you must gracefully give up the thrill of finding that one rare, golden seed that grows a hundredfold (the multi-bagger). You will learn why surrendering the absolute highest peaks of direct profit is often the necessary price for a peaceful night's sleep.

The Magic of the SIP (Systematic Investment Plan): How the simple act of planting one small seed every single month transforms ordinary income into an unstoppable financial fortress.

The Eighth Wonder of the World: The quiet, breathtaking power of Compounding—where your money begins to make its own money, turning steady, risk-adjusted returns into generational wealth.

You do not need to be a fearless stock-picker to build an empire of wealth. You just need the discipline to start planting.

The journey of the Awakening Investor continues soon.

www.ingramcontent.com/pod-product-compliance
Lightning Source LLC
LaVergne TN
LVHW090330210926
848480LV00004B/1359